Helping Children See Jesus

ISBN: 978-1-64104-027-3

Godliness
Old Testament Volume 21:
1 Samuel Part 2

Author: Arlene S. Piepgrass
Illustrator: Vernon Henkel
Colorization Courtesy of Good Life Ministries
Page Layout: Patricia Pope

© 2021 Bible Visuals International
PO Box 153, Akron, PA 17501-0153
Phone: (717) 859-1131
www.biblevisuals.org

All rights reserved. No part of this publication may be reproduced, stored in a retrieval system or transmitted in any form by any means, electronic, mechanical, photocopy, recording or otherwise, without the prior permission of the publisher, except as provided by USA copyright law.

RELATED ITEMS

To access related items (such as activities, memory verse posters and translated texts) please visit our web store at www.biblevisuals.org and enter 2021 at the top right of the web page. You may need to reduce the zoom setting to get the search box.

FREE TEXT DOWNLOAD

To obtain a FREE printable copy of the English teaching text (PDF format) under Product Format, please scroll down and select Extra–PDF Teacher Text Download. Then under Language select English before clicking the ADD TO CART button to place in your shopping cart. Other languages are available at an additional cost from the Language menu. When checking out, use coupon code XTACSV17 at checkout and click on Apply Coupon to receive the discount on the English text.

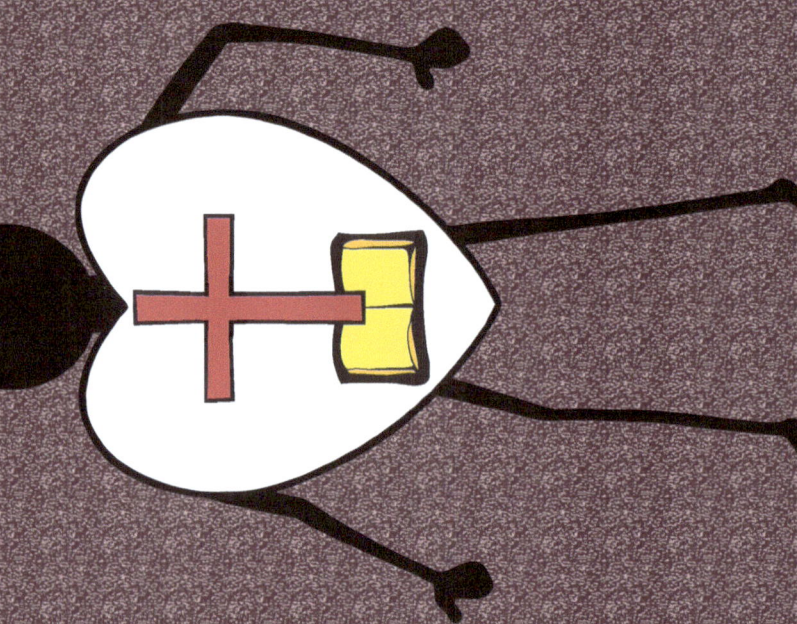

The LORD seeth not as man seeth; for man looketh on the outward appearance, but the LORD looketh on the heart. 1 Samuel 16:7b

Lesson 1
GOD CHOOSES A GODLY MAN AS KING

NOTE TO THE TEACHER

If possible, use this series of lessons right after teaching Old Testament Volume 20 *Disobedience*. Your students should have the historical background given in Volume 20. Then they will understand the events in this series. If you cannot use the lessons on *Disobedience*, give your students a brief summary of Saul's failure (1 Samuel 13:1-15:35). Make it clear that as a result of Saul's disobedience God rejected him as king.

On a large card print the word GODLINESS. Hold it up for the class at the beginning of this lesson, and whenever you use the word in this series. *Godliness* means "devotion to God". A godly person behaves right. He has a right attitude toward God and others. He is eager to obey the will of God.

Your students will enjoy studying the map to see the movement in these lessons.

BACKGROUND

King Saul was a fearful, jealous, angry man–because he disobeyed God. Instead of honoring God, he became self-centered. So God chose David to replace Saul (1 Samuel 16:13-14). Saul's reign continued for 32 years. Because King Saul was willfully disobedient, he did not enjoy God's presence or power. Finally God removed him from the throne by death.

But David was being prepared by God to replace Saul. David is described as a man after God's own heart (1 Samuel 13:14). He was not perfect. But his heart was usually right toward the Lord. He demonstrated what God can do through one who is surrendered to Him.

These lessons cover a period of about 15 years. The events occurred about 1,000 years before Christ Jesus was born.

Scripture to be studied: 1 Samuel 16

The *aim* of the lesson: To show the kind of person God approves and uses.

What your students should *know*: That the Lord sees your heart–your innermost self.

What your students should *feel*: The desire for a heart attitude which pleases God.

What your students should *do*: Confess to the Lord everything which displeases Him. Ask God's forgiveness and accept His cleansing from sin.

Lesson outline (for the teacher's and students' notebooks):

1. God sends Samuel to meet the king He had chosen (1 Samuel 16:1-12).
2. God knew David's heart (Psalm 14:1; 8:3, 6; 139:1-12; 51:1-19; 37:3-5; 100:1-5; 61:1-4).
3. Samuel anoints David as king (1 Samuel 16:13).
4. David serves Saul (1 Samuel 16:14-23).

The verse to be memorized:

The LORD seeth not as man seeth; for man looketh on the outward appearance, but the LORD looketh on the heart.
(1 Samuel 16:7b)

THE LESSON

Saul was not a godly man. He deliberately *chose* to disobey God. No one forced him to be disobedient. He himself made the choice. Saul was the first man to rule as king over the Israelite people. Who was their King before Saul? (*God*) Why did God not continue to be their King? (*Israel wanted a man for their king–like all the other nations.*) God gave them their wish. He chose Saul to be their human king.

If Saul had obeyed God, he could have had a wonderful life, filled with God's blessing. Instead, he *deliberately disobeyed* God. (See 1 Samuel 13:9-14; 15:1-23.)

Samuel, God's prophet, announced God's judgment to Saul: "The Lord has chosen *a man after His [God's] own heart* [a godly man] to be king in your place" (1 Samuel 13:14; 15:28).

(*Teacher:* Help your students to describe "a man after God's heart." *One who believes God's Word, is obedient to God, kind, loving, honest, humble, patient, truthful, one who does good deeds*)

Today I brought an egg to class. By looking at it, can you tell whether it is soft or hard inside? Can you tell if it is good or rotten? Why not? (*Because we can see only the outside, not the inside*)

(*Teacher:* Ask a student to volunteer to stand before the class. Describe some of his/her positive outward traits.)

Can you see inside him/her and tell what (s)he is thinking? (*No*) Who can see into his heart to know whether or not he/she loves God? (*God alone. We can see only the outside of one another.*) Read and discuss 1 Samuel 16:7b.

1. GOD SENDS SAMUEL TO MEET THE KING HE HAD CHOSEN
1 Samuel 16:1-12

Samuel was sad that Saul would not obey God. He sometimes cried when he thought about it. He was sorry that Saul had turned away from God and refused to obey Him.

One day God spoke to Samuel saying, "You have mourned long enough for Saul. I have rejected him as king. I want you to go to Bethlehem. Take a heifer [young cow] with you and offer it as a sacrifice to Me. Invite the man named Jesse to join you at the sacrifice. I have chosen one of the sons of Jesse to be the next king. I will show you which one."

When Samuel arrived at Bethlehem the leaders of the city were frightened. "Have we done something wrong?" they asked. "Why have you come here?"

They knew Samuel was a prophet through whom God spoke to the people.

"Don't be afraid," Samuel told the trembling men. "You have done nothing wrong. I want to offer a sacrifice to God. Will you join me? But first, tell me where Jesse is."

"He's right over there," one of the leaders answered.

Samuel called Jesse. "Will you join me in the sacrifice?" he asked. "Bring your sons, too, so we all can worship God together."

Preparations were made. Soon the people began to gather for the time of worship. Who do you think Samuel was especially eager to see? (*Jesse's sons*)

– 19 –

Show Illustration #1

Jesse proudly presented his eldest son. "Samuel, this is Eliab, my firstborn," he said.

Samuel studied Eliab. He thought to himself, *What a handsome man, tall and erect! He would be a fine king for Israel.*

God knew what Samuel was thinking. Quickly God whispered to Samuel: "No! He is not My choice. He *is* tall and handsome. But that is not important." (Quote 1 Samuel 16:7b.)

Next Jesse introduced another son, Abinadab. Samuel shook his head. Then Shammah was presented. "He is not the one," God told Samuel.

In all, seven sons of Jesse were introduced to Samuel. Each time God said, "No."

Samuel was puzzled. He asked, "Jesse, are all your sons here?"

"I have one more named David," Jesse answered. "But he is very young. He is taking care of the sheep."

"Please send for him at once," ordered Samuel. "We will not begin the sacrifice until he comes."

"When David appeared, God whispered to Samuel, "David is My choice. He is a man after My own heart. He will be the next king."

2. GOD KNEW DAVID'S HEART
Psalm 14:1; 8:3, 6; 139:1-12; 51:1-19; 37:3-5; 100:1-5; 61:1-4

David, *a man after God's own heart*. (Have students repeat 1 Samuel 16:7b.) This means God knew David's thoughts. He knew Whom David loved most. God alone knew what David was *really* like.

Would you like to know what God saw in David's heart?

1. He saw that David *believed* in God. (Read slowly Psalm 14:1; 53:1. Encourage students to explain the meaning.) Some people are not sure if there is a God. Others *are* sure there is *no* God. What does God call such people? (*Fools.*)

    David believed that God was the *Creator* of all the universe (Psalm 8:3-6, 19:1-6).

    David believed that God is *omniscient (He knows everything*, Psalm 139:1-6).

    David believed that God is *omnipresent (present everywhere, all the time*, Psalm 139:7-12). No one can hide from God.

    What do *you* believe about God? He knows what you are thinking. You cannot deceive God.

2. Looking inside David, God saw a *repentant* heart (Psalm 51). David wasn't perfect. He sinned when he was young and would sin when he was older. But whenever he sinned, he was truly sorry. Each time he asked God to forgive him. And the Lord did pardon him.

    God wants you, too, to tell Him when you have done wrong. If you are genuinely sorry for your sin, He will forgive you. (See Proverbs 28:13, 1 John 1:9.)

3. God saw that David had a *trusting* heart (Psalm 37:3-5, 46:10, 31:14). David didn't always understand the things that happened to him. But he knew God was doing what was best. Even when he was afraid, he trusted in God (Psalm 56:3). Are you ever afraid? This is a good verse for you to quote at such times.

4. God saw that David had a *thankful* heart (Psalm 100:1-5, 75:1; 92:1-5; 106:1). When David thought about God, he remembered the love of God. Also, David had experienced God's protection, His provision, His power. Over and over again he praised the Lord and thanked Him. He said, "My mouth shall praise the Lord all the time!" (Psalm 34:1-3). How do you use your mouth? (Let students respond.) How much better to praise the Lord than to grumble, tattle or find fault with others. (Read Psalm 50:23a aloud.)

5. God saw David's *dependent* heart (Psalm 46:1-2; 61:1-4). David knew that day and night he needed God's help in protecting his sheep.

Show Illustration #2

Sometimes the lions and bears attacked his flock. David quickly breathed a prayer: "Dear Lord, please help me kill this beast." And God answered David's prayer.

Is school work hard for you? Do some people tell lies about you? Is it hard to obey your parents or the person you work for? (Let students suggest their problems.) If you will let Him, God will help you just as He helped David. Tell the Lord your problems. Depend on His help every moment of every day.

When God looked inside David's heart, He didn't see a *perfect* man. But He saw one who loved the Lord and wanted to please Him. He was a God-like man. (Show sign: GODLINESS.) So the Lord chose David to be the next king of the Israelites. God knew David would try to lead the people wisely.

3. SAMUEL ANOINTS DAVID AS KING
1 Samuel 16:13

The Lord knew everything about David. He told Samuel, "This is the man I have chosen."

Show Illustration #3

At once Samuel poured olive oil on David's head.

At that moment, something happened deep in David's heart. He understood that God had chosen him to be king. God's Word says, "The Spirit of the Lord came mightily upon David from that day forward." (See 1 Samuel 16:13.) Young David wouldn't be able to rule without help. Therefore the Lord gave His power to David for the great task which would be his some day.

David went back to the field to care for his sheep. He was young and inexperienced. He needed to learn many lessons from God before becoming king.

4. DAVID SERVES SAUL
1 Samuel 16:14-23

While David cared for his sheep, King Saul still reigned. (Repeat 1 Samuel 16:7b.)

Would you like to know what God saw in Saul's heart?

1. Saul had a *disobedient* heart (1 Samuel 13:8-14; 15:9).
2. Saul had a *dishonest* heart (1 Samuel 15:3-14). He lied, saying he had done what God had commanded.

3. Saul had an *unrepentant* heart (1 Samuel 15:15-21). Instead of confessing his wrongdoing when Samuel pointed it out, he made excuses for himself. He blamed others rather than admitting he was wrong.
4. Saul had a *rebellious* heart (1 Samuel 15:21-23). He rejected the Word of the Lord.

Saul was a handsome man (1 Samuel 10:23-24). He looked like a king. But when God looked into his heart, He saw He could not use Saul (1 Samuel 13:14; 15:23).

When Saul had been anointed king, the Spirit of God had come upon him. God's Spirit gave him the ability to be a good, obedient king (1 Samuel 10:9). But Saul rejected God, and the Spirit of God left him (1 Samuel 16:14a).

Saul became miserable. God allowed an evil spirit to torment Saul, making him sad and fearful (1 Samuel 16:14b-15). Saul often had fits of anger. His attendants watched him closely. But they couldn't help him.

One day a servant made a suggestion. "O King! Let us find someone who can play the harp. Then when you are sad and afraid, the music will help you to feel better."

"That is a good idea," said the king. "Do you know a harpist?"

"Yes, there is a young shepherd. He lives in Bethlehem," the servant answered. "I know his father, Jesse. I believe he would let David come to the palace to help you."

"Send for him at once," Saul ordered.

And that is how David came to the palace. God–the omnipotent One–had arranged it in this most unexpected way! Saul didn't know that God had chosen David to be the next king.

Saul liked David very much. He soon asked Jesse if his son, David, could stay in the palace. Saul wanted David to be his armor-bearer (bodyguard).

Show Illustration #4

So David lived in the palace. Every time Saul was tormented by the evil spirit, David played his harp. He also sang songs about God, the faithful One. The evil spirit would go away then, and the king felt better.

If Saul had turned to God for help and forgiveness, he would have enjoyed life. Instead, he no longer listened to the Lord. He went his own sinful way. So he was extremely unhappy. How different Saul's heart was from David's heart!

Today, when others look at you, they see your face and your clothes. But when God looks at you, He sees inside your heart. Does He see a heart like Saul's? If so, confess your sin and disobedience to Him. He will forgive you and cleanse your heart. (See Proverbs 28:13, 1 John 1:9.)

Or does God see inside you a heart like David's–full of godliness? (Show GODLINESS sign.) Are you trusting in the Lord Jesus Christ as your Saviour? Does He see in you a heart that wants to please God?

God could use David as His servant because his heart pleased God. He was a *godly* young man. (Show GODLINESS sign.) God wants you to be godly, too. He wants you to obey Him. Only then can He use you. Will you choose to live a godly life?

Lesson 2
GODLINESS PREPARES A MAN FOR RESPONSIBILITY

NOTE TO THE TEACHER

Some 400 years before the events of this lesson, the Israelites moved into Palestine. God had commanded them to destroy the wicked nations living in the land. He charged His people not to marry the foreigners there. He did not want His people to get involved with them. (See Deuteronomy 7.) The Israelites failed to obey the Lord. Consequently, they were continually threatened by their enemies in the land.

During the years of the Judges, several enemy nations enslaved God's people. At the time of the book of First Samuel, the Israelites were often overcome by the Philistines. Again and again God miraculously delivered the Israelites. But each time the enemy came back again. The Israelites should have boldly claimed God's help to march against the Philistine army. Instead, they were terrified and trembling, seeing only their own weakness (1 Samuel 17:24). Happily, God worked a mighty miracle through a godly young man–David. David was completely yielded to Him.

At the beginning of the lesson, review the meaning of GODLINESS, holding up the sign before your students.

Scripture to be studied: 1 Samuel 17:1-58; 18:6-30

The *aim* of the lesson: To show that David's daily faithfulness to God prepared him for the challenge of Goliath.

What your students should *know*: That David *knew* God was his Helper.

What your students should *feel*: Certain that God will help them to obey Him.

What your students should *do*: Turn to God for help in difficult situations.

Lesson outline (for the teacher's and students' notebooks):
1. Goliath challenges the Israelites (1 Samuel 17:1-10).
2. David accepts Goliath's challenge (1 Samuel 17:11-40).
3. David defeats Goliath (1 Samuel 17:41-58).
4. Saul becomes jealous of David (1 Samuel 18:6-30).

The verse to be memorized:

The LORD seeth not as man seeth; for man looketh on the outward appearance, but the LORD looketh on the heart.
(1 Samuel 16:7b)

THE LESSON

David lived a life of godliness. Is godliness helpful? et's find out!

Have you ever had someone who always fought against you? Was he bigger and stronger than you? Did he try to throw you to the ground?

The Israelites had such an enemy–the Philistines. The Philistines wanted to conquer the people of Israel and rule over them. There had been times when God performed miracles to help the Israelites defeat the Philistines. (See 1 Samuel 14:12-23; 7:7-14.) But each time the enemy trained new soldiers and returned to fight the men of Israel.

1. GOLIATH CHALLENGES THE ISRAELITES
1 Samuel 17:1-10

The Philistine army was ready for another battle. They lined up on a hill overlooking a small stream winding through the valley below. Their weapons and armor flashed in the morning sun. The Israelite army, led by King Saul, was camped on the opposite hill. A broad valley separated the two armies.

Thump, thump, thump! The earth seemed to shake. It was early morning. Were the Philistines marching toward the men of Israel? No! Down in the valley only one soldier stomped back and forth.

Show Illustration #5

Thump, thump, thump! That soldier was huge–much, much taller than any Israelite soldier. He was over 9½ feet tall! (*Teacher:* Show, by comparison, how tall he was. For example, "His head would have reached _____ .") He was Goliath, a *giant*!

Goliath wore a heavy bronze armor. How could anyone kill him with a spear? (On illustration #5 point out the helmet, armor, bronze leggings.)

Look at his spear! Listen to Goliath! His shouts sound like thunder. Listen!

"Where is the man who dares to fight me? I am a Philistine. You are the servants of Saul. Why should all the men in our armies go to war? Send only one man to fight me. If he kills me, all the Philistines will be your slaves. But, if I kill him, all you Israelites will be our slaves. Come on! Send me a man!"

Thump, thump, thump! Goliath tramped back and forth.

The Israelite soldiers were terrified and scrambled farther up the hill (1 Samuel 17:24). Not one volunteered to meet Goliath on the battlefield. Each feared that to do so would mean instant death.

What had the Israelites forgotten? (*God was on their side.*) Read Deuteronomy 20:1-4 slowly. The men of Israel studied their own small, poorly equipped army. What a contrast to the overpowering army of the Philistines! The Israelites had forgotten that the Lord God had previously defeated the Philistines. (See 1 Samuel 14:23; 7:13.)

Poor King Saul! He didn't ask God to help him. Instead he announced, "The man who defeats this giant will have my daughter for his wife. And I will make him rich. And his family will never have to pay taxes!"

The news spread throughout the Israelite camp. What wonderful rewards for a brave soldier!

But no one–not one soldier–was brave enough to fight Goliath!

2. DAVID ACCEPTS GOLIATH'S CHALLENGE
1 Samuel 17:11-40

Three of David's older brothers were soldiers in the Israelite army. They heard Goliath's proud challenge every morning and evening. They wanted King Saul's rewards. But like the rest of the men in the army, they were too terrified to face the giant.

One day these three men had a surprise. Their youngest brother, David, ran to them on the battle line.

"David! What are you doing here?" the three demanded.

"Our father sent you some bread and cheese and corn," David answered. "He wants to know if you are safe and well."

Thump, thump, thump! What was that? (Let students respond.) Why was everyone scared? (Allow response.)

Again Goliath bellowed as before. (Repeat threats.)

David turned to the soldiers near him. "Why does that Philistine defy the army of the living God?" David asked. "Why doesn't someone kill him? It is a disgrace to the people of God! What will the king do for the man who fights and kills him?" (Let students answer David's question.)

"How long has Goliath been doing this?" David wanted to know.

"Every morning and evening for 40 days!" the soldiers answered.

"Forty days!" David exclaimed. "Tell King Saul that I'll go out and fight that giant! He can't talk this wickedly and get away with it."

Eliab, David's oldest brother, grabbed David angrily. "Why have you come down here?" he raged. "Why didn't you stay home with your sheep? Who do you think you are? You're no soldier! How can you fight a giant? You're only a shepherd!"

Shaking loose from Eliab, David turned to the other soldiers. "I *will* fight that giant!" David announced. "He has no right to threaten us and scorn our God!"

Word of all this reached King Saul. Immediately he sent for David.

Show Illustration #6

Saul stared at the young shepherd who had no armor, no sword, no shield.

Before the king said a word, David spoke. "Don't be discouraged because of this wicked Philistine, O King! I am your servant. I will fight him."

"But you are young," King Saul said. "You are no match for Goliath. You have no experience. He has fought for years. And do you know how tall he is?"

"O King Saul," David replied confidently, "a lion and a bear attacked my sheep. But God helped me to kill both of them. I *know* He will help me kill this wicked man. He has no right to jeer at the army of the living God. The Lord will give me the victory just as He helped me kill the lion and the bear."

For years David had trusted in the living God. And God had been preparing him for this day. David was a *godly* young man. His *godliness* (Show GODLINESS sign.) caused him to depend on the Lord. Now he was ready to accept the challenge of Goliath.

"David, you are brave," said King Saul. "Here, put on my armor. May the Lord God be with you."

David drooped in Saul's heavy armor. He couldn't move! "I can't fight in this!" David exclaimed and wriggled out of the armor.

"You'll be killed without it!" Saul shouted. But David had already headed for the battlefield.

3. DAVID DEFEATS GOLIATH
1 Samuel 17:41-58

Thump, thump! thump! The earth shook as Goliath tramped back and forth. "Send me a man to fight!" he thundered. "Send a man to fight me!"

The Philistines and the Israelites saw young David running toward Goliath. He skidded to a stop at a brook. There he chose five smooth stones and put them into his shepherd's bag. Then, with his sling in his hand, he went straight toward Goliath.

When Goliath saw that David had no weapons and no armor, he was wild. "Do you think I am a dog that you can fight with sticks?" he bellowed. "Come here to me. I shall give your body to the birds and beasts to eat!" And Goliath cursed David in the names of his heathen gods.

(*Teacher:* Read David's answer in 1 Samuel 17:45-47 forcefully. Emphasize: "I come to you in the name of the Lord of hosts . . . . The Lord will deliver you into my hands . . . . All the earth will know that there is a God in Israel . . . The battle is the Lord's.")

"The Lord will help me kill you! Our army will defeat your army!" David shouted. "Today the birds and beasts will eat your body, not mine!"

The giant thumped! thumped! thumped! towards David. On the run, David snatched a stone from his bag, placed it in his sling, whirled it round and round and let it fly. Swish!

With a great thud, Goliath fell on his face to the ground! That little stone had sunk into Goliath's forehead!

Show Illustration #7

David ran and stood over Goliath, grabbed the giant's sword and cut off his head!

The Philistine soldiers were terrified. Did they surrender? Did they become slaves of the Israelites as Goliath had promised? No! They turned and ran in every direction.

The Israelite soldiers shouted triumphantly. They chased the Philistines, killing as many as they could.

Exactly as David had said, the Lord conquered the Philistines. He proved to the Israelites and the Philistines that the living and true *God of Israel gives victory*.

God chose to use David, a *godly* (show GODLINESS sign) youth who trusted the Lord for victory. The Lord was preparing young David for even greater responsibility.

4. SAUL BECOMES JEALOUS OF DAVID
1 Samuel 18:6-30

News of David's victory spread quickly. When King Saul and his soldiers returned from the battle, people thronged along the roadside. Listen to what they were singing. (Read 1 Samuel 18:6-7.) Who was getting more praise? (*David.*) How do you think Saul felt? Was he pleased that David had killed Goliath? (Let students discuss.)

Have you ever been jealous of anyone? How does jealousy make you feel? (Have a discussion, emphasizing that hatred and revenge result from jealousy.)

Saul was furious. He thought, *I hate David! He is more popular than I am. Soon the people will want to make him king in my place! I will kill him!*

Show Illustration #8

The next day, David tried to calm the king by playing his harp. Suddenly Saul hurled his spear at David. David dodged and was safe. Another day Saul again tried to kill David–and failed a second time.

Later Saul had another idea. He called David and said, "My daughter Michal loves you. If you will kill 100 Philistines, you can be my son-in-law."

To himself, Saul said, *Now I'll get rid of David. He will be killed by the Philistines. And I will no longer need to worry about his popularity*!

David and his men went out at once. When he returned he reported, "I have killed *200* Philistines!" Saul was amazed that David was safe. But he kept his word and David married the king's daughter.

Why do you think David was successful in everything he did? (*The Lord God helped him.*) Why was Saul unable to kill David? (*God protected David.*) What had the Lord planned for David's life? (*He was to become the next king.*)

How could Saul have overcome his jealousy and hatred? (*By turning to God for help*) Instead, he turned away from God.

Are you like David or Saul? Are you a godly person, or do you turn your back on God? Do you depend on the Lord to help you each day? Or do you try to live without God?

Today, will you turn to the Lord and ask His help in your daily life? If you are not a child of God, will you receive His salvation from sin?

Lesson 3
GODLINESS, THE FOUNDATION OF FRIENDSHIP

NOTE TO THE TEACHER

Friendship is a gift from God. The relationship between David and Jonathan shows the blessing of godly friendship.

Emphasize: (1) The importance of choosing friends who love God; (2) The importance of being a friend who loves God.

Our best Friend is the Lord Jesus Christ.

Your alert students may question why God permitted lying. (Lies and idolatry marred Michal's character: 1 Samuel 19:14-17. Jonathan and David were untruthful: 1 Samuel 20:5-6, 27-29.) God did not deal with these lies. But He *always* hates sin.

If these three people had been perfectly truthful, the final outcome would have been even more miraculous.

Begin the lesson by reviewing the meaning of godliness, holding up the sign. GODLINESS affects our relationship with God and with people.

Scripture to be studied: 1 Samuel 18:1-4; 19:1-10; 20:1-42

The *aim* of the lesson: To show the blessing of a godly friendship.

What your students should *know*: The importance of choosing godly friends.

What your students should *feel*: The desire to be a godly friend to others.

What your students should *do*: Check to be sure their friendships please God.

Lesson outline (for the teacher's and students' notebooks):
1. God gives David a friend (1 Samuel 18:1-4).
2. David is defended by his friend (1 Samuel 19:1-18).
3. David is warned by his friend (1 Samuel 20:1-42).
4. David and Jonathan pledge their friendship (1 Samuel 20:12-17, 23, 42).

The verse to be memorized:

The LORD seeth not as man seeth; for man looketh on the outward appearance, but the LORD looketh on the heart.
(1 Samuel 16:7b)

THE LESSON

Godliness is very important in a Christian's life. It even affects friendships, as we shall see in this lesson.

What is a friend? Do you have a special friend? How would you describe a *good* friend? (Encourage discussion.)

Here are the Bible's descriptions of a friend: "A friend loves at all times" (Proverbs 17:17). "A friend sticks closer than a brother" (Proverbs 18:24b). A friend will stick with you no matter what happens. (See Proverbs 27:6a.) A sincere friend will always be honest with you. Sometimes a friend must point out where you are wrong. That same friend will give you wise advice. (See Proverbs 27:6.)

A real friend will love you. Trusted friends are loyal, patient, kind and unselfish. A true friend is not jealous of you but is happy when you succeed. (See 1 Corinthians 13:4-7.)

1. GOD GIVES DAVID A FRIEND
1 Samuel 18:1-4

Was King Saul a good friend to David? (Discuss.) When Saul was upset, he was glad David played the harp for him. He was delighted when David was courageous enough to kill Goliath. But he hated David. Why? (Let students discuss Saul's jealousy.) Saul was so jealous of David that he wanted to kill him. He was not a true friend. Saul was David's enemy.

King Saul had a son named Jonathan. Prince Jonathan was a soldier in his father's army. But Jonathan wasn't like his father. Jonathan loved God very much. Before David killed Goliath, Jonathan and his armor-bearer battled the Philistines. (See 1 Samuel 14:1-15.) Jonathan asked God to show him what to do. He trusted God to help him. And God caused Jonathan to defeat the Philistines. Jonathan gave glory to God for that victory.

Jonathan had seen David kill Goliath. He heard David give all the praise to God. Jonathan doubtless thought, *I would like to know David. I want him for a friend. He is brave and–best of all–he loves God.*

Jonathan, the prince, expected to become king after the death of his father, King Saul. David was only a poor shepherd. But that did not matter to Jonathan.

A day came when Jonathan and David were alone. "David," Jonathan began, "I want to be your friend. I know you love God. You also love our nation. You want to protect our people from our enemies. I'll be your friend always and will do all I can to help you."

Show Illustration #9

Jonathan took off his princely robe and put it on David. He gave David his armor. Did Jonathan realize that the Lord had chosen David, not himself, to be the next king? We don't know, but we *do* know that Jonathan wasn't jealous of David. Instead he honored David above himself.

2. DAVID IS DEFENDED BY HIS FRIEND
1 Samuel 19:1-18

After David had killed Goliath, King Saul kept him in his army. Everyone loved him. (See 1 Samuel 18:5, 16, 30.) Whenever David fought a battle, he defeated the enemy. Why? (Let students answer. Read 1 Samuel 18:14.)

How do you think Saul felt about this? (Discuss. Read 1 Samuel 18:29.) What do you suppose Saul did? (Read 1 Samuel 19:1.) Did Jonathan obey his father? (Give opportunity for response.) What would you have done if you were Jonathan? (Discuss.)

First, Jonathan told David: "My father wants to kill you. You must hide while I coax him to change his mind. You're my best friend, David. I'll do all I can to help you." (See 1 Samuel 19:2-3.)

Show Illustration #10

– 24 –

The next morning Jonathan went to King Saul. "Father, why do you want to kill David?" he asked. "He's done nothing to harm you. He's always helped you in every way possible. Remember how he risked his life to kill Goliath? God used Him to give us a great victory over the Philistines. You were so happy that day. You don't want to kill an innocent man, do you?"

King Saul thought a bit. Then he said, "You are right, Jonathan my son. As the Lord lives, David will not be put to death."

Imagine how happy Jonathan was when he met and talked with David! "You can come back to the palace. My father won't kill you. You'll be safe, David."

Together they went to the palace. Life returned to normal. Whenever David fought the Philistines, he defeated them. He often played his harp for King Saul. Everything seemed fine.

But Saul hated it when David was successful and popular. King Saul thought, *David is going to take the kingdom from me. I hate him. I will not let him take my throne. I will kill him!* (*Teacher:* Emphasize that our thoughts control us and our actions.)

Such thoughts made Saul even more angry. One night David was playing his harp for the king. Suddenly Saul flung his spear at him. David dodged quickly, just in time. A second later, he would have been pinned to the wall.

David dashed from the palace. At home he told his wife, Michal, "I can't stay at the palace any longer. I can't trust King Saul. He says he won't kill me. But again today he hurled his spear at me. It's not safe for me to be there."

Michal loved David very much. She didn't want Saul, her father, to kill him. Then she learned that the king had sent two men to watch their house. They were commanded to kill David the next morning. Quickly she warned David: "You must leave immediately! Hurry! I'll let you down through this window. Then run! I'll take care of the king's messengers." As soon as David was gone, Michal grabbed a big idol and put it in the bed. She covered the idol to make it look like David.

In the morning the messengers knocked on the door. "We have come to take David to the king."

"Oh, I am sorry," Michal answered. "David is sick and can't go with you."

When the king heard this, he demanded that they bring David in his bed. Imagine their surprise when they found the idol in the bed! Think of King Saul's fury!

This had given David time to escape. He ran to Ramah where Samuel, his friend, was staying. David needed someone to whom he could tell his fears.

David knew also how to call out to God. Listen to David's prayer. (*Teacher:* Psalm 59 is David's prayer at this time. Read verses 1-4 and 16-17. David trusted in God even in great danger. He asked God for His protection and deliverance. He thanked God for His strength, His safe-keeping and His love.)

Had you been with King Saul that day, how would you have advised him? (*Pray to God for help. Confess your sin. Seek forgiveness. Ask David's forgiveness.*) Saul never asked God's forgiveness. He desperately wanted to find David and kill him.

3. DAVID IS WARNED BY HIS FRIEND
1 Samuel 20:1-42

In time, David secretly met with Jonathan. "Jonathan," David began, "what have I done wrong? Why is your father determined to kill me?"

"Oh, David, he won't kill you," comforted Jonathan. "He tells me everything. And he hasn't said anything about killing you. Trust me, David. You're my true friend."

"Jonathan, that is exactly the reason he wouldn't tell you. He knows we're friends. He knows you would tell me. But, Jonathan, I'm only one step from death!" David exclaimed.

David was worried. He had reason to be worried. But he had better reasons to *not* worry. God had chosen him to be the next king. Samuel had anointed him. Surely God would protect him, even if Saul did try to kill him. But David had forgotten this. He was looking at his dreadful circumstances.

Jonathan knew that David was terrified. He asked, "David, what do you want me to do for you?"

Listen carefully to David's plan. (Read slowly 1 Samuel 20:5-7.)

"I'll be eager to hear what your father says. Please be honest with me, Jonathan," David begged.

"You can trust me, David," Jonathan replied. "We have pledged our friendship. I will not betray you."

"How will I learn how your father really feels towards me?"

"Come with me," said Jonathan. "I have a plan. You can count on me." What a good friend Jonathan was! He helped David when he needed it most.

Walking into the field together, Jonathan explained his plan. "Do you see that pile of stones over there? Come back three days from now and hide behind them. A boy and I will come out here. I'll bring my arrows. I will shoot three arrows as though I am shooting a target. I may shout to the boy, 'They're on this side!' If so, you'll know it's safe for you to come back to the palace. But if I shout, 'Go farther! They're beyond you,' you will know my father plans to kill you. So run away fast!"

Jonathan was really the kind of friend we read about in Proverbs. He loved David at all times. He was even more faithful to David than a brother.

Jonathan returned to the palace. He was certain he could persuade his father to be kind to David. The next day Jonathan ate with King Saul and those from his court. David's place at the table was empty. Saul said nothing.

Again, the second day David's place was empty. With a scowl, Saul asked Jonathan, "Where is David?" Let's read together what Jonathan told his father. (Read 1 Samuel 20:28-29.)

When Saul heard this, he flew into a rage. "Jonathan! You know you cannot be king as long as David lives. Go get him at once so I can kill him!" he screamed.

"But what has he done? Why should he be killed?" asked Jonathan. Jonathan thought his father would turn from his wicked desire to murder David. Instead, Saul was so furious that he hurled his spear at Jonathan to kill him. But Jonathan dodged and escaped.

Angrily, Jonathan left, knowing his good friend was in danger. David could not return to the palace. How he would miss him!

The next day David was hiding behind the stones as planned. His heart pounded wildly. He thought, *What will the answer be? Can I return to the palace? I enjoy serving the king. I like leading his soldiers in battle. If only King Saul realized I am not trying to take his throne from him. Jonathan is a splendid friend. How good it is to serve with him!*

That moment David saw a boy and Jonathan coming with bow and arrow.

Show Illustration #11

Swish! Swish! Swish! Three arrows flew from Jonathan's bow. Jonathan shouted to the boy, "Go farther! The arrows are beyond you."

David was broken-hearted. He now knew he had to flee for his life. To return to the palace would mean certain death.

Jonathan sent the boy back to the palace. Then David came out of hiding. He ran to Jonathan, threw his arms around him and sobbed.

4. DAVID AND JONATHAN PLEDGE THEIR FRIENDSHIP
1 Samuel 20:12-17, 23, 42

Finally, Jonathan said, "David, we must now separate. But remember the promises we made to each other!"

"I will never forget them, Jonathan," David promised. "I shall always have love for–and show kindness to–you and your children."

"Will you remember this even when you become king?" Jonathan asked.

"I will never forget, Jonathan," David assured him. "You are a wonderful friend. Even if I never see you again, I will always remember our agreement."

"Good-bye, David," Jonathan said sadly. "You must go. And I must return to the palace."

Show Illustration #12

After quickly embracing each other they parted. David called, "Jonathan, I won't forget my promise." And he didn't.

What kind of a friend are you to others? Are you like Jonathan–godly, loyal, unselfish?

Why is it important for us to choose friends who love God? (*We are influenced by our friends. If they do what pleases the Lord, they will help us do right.*)

Who is our best Friend? (*The Lord Jesus Christ*) He loved us so much He died for us. (See John 3:16; Romans 5:8.) He was so unselfish that He left the palace of Heaven and came to earth for us. (See Philippians 2:5-8.) He promised never to leave those who receive Him as Saviour (Hebrews 13:5).

We were doomed to death (Romans 6:23a). But we have a Friend and Saviour who died in our place and provided a way of escape for us (Romans 6:23b). If He is not your Saviour and Friend, will you receive Him today? (See John 1:12.)

Lesson 4
GODLINESS PRODUCES KINDNESS

Scripture to be studied: 1 Samuel 21-2 Samuel 1

The *aim* of the lesson: To show that a right relationship to God makes us kind to others–even our enemies.

What your students should *know*: That godliness does not mean a person is perfect.

What your students should *feel*: A desire to show kindness even to those who are unkind to them.

What your students should *do*: Think about their attitudes towards those who mistreat them. Ask God to change wrong attitudes.

Lesson outline (for the teacher's and students' notebooks):
1. David runs away (1 Samuel 21-22).
2. God protects David (1 Samuel 23).
3. David loves his enemy (1 Samuel 24 and 26).
4. David mourns (1 Samuel 31; 2 Samuel 1).

The verse to be memorized:

The LORD seeth not as man seeth; for man looketh on the outward appearance, but the LORD looketh on the heart.
(1 Samuel 16:7b)

THE LESSON

Can you pretend you are David? Answer these questions as you think David would answer them if he were here.

David, why are you afraid? (*Because Saul is trying to kill me.*)

NOTE TO THE TEACHER

It is impossible to include in one lesson all that is covered in 1 Samuel 21 through 2 Samuel 1. However, please be sure to read all these chapters. Only then can you understand the sequence of events. The sections selected for these lessons emphasize the doctrine of godliness.

Hold up the printed poster with the word GODLINESS. Review the meaning. Remember:

1. Godliness affects our relationship with God.
2. Godliness affects our friendships.
3. Godliness shines best when shown to those who are unkind and hateful.

David, why is Saul trying to kill you? (*I am more popular than he is. The people love me. Saul is jealous of me. He thinks I want to replace him as king.*)

David, do you want to kill Saul so you can be king? (*No! I simply want to serve the king in the palace with my friend, Jonathan.*)

David, are you going back to the palace? (*No. I am not safe there.*)

David is afraid because he has forgotten something important. What has he forgotten? (*David was chosen by God to be the next king. Surely God will protect him.*)

David was in danger, and he was afraid. He loved God very much, but he did not always depend on Him.

1. DAVID RUNS AWAY
1 Samuel 21-22

David knew that the people loved him. He knew they gave him more honor than they gave Saul. (See 1 Samuel 18:7, 30.) He could have gathered an army and gone to war against Saul. But God had chosen Saul to be the first king of Israel. So, David had respect for Saul.

What should David have done to escape Saul's anger? (*Asked God to direct him*) Instead, he made his own plans. He decided to hide so Saul couldn't find him. First he ran to a town called Nob. Many priests lived there and served God in the tabernacle. Ahimelech was the high priest. He was terrified when he saw David coming.

David tried to calm him. "Do not be afraid, Ahimelech," David said. "The king has sent me on urgent business. I need some bread and a spear or a sword."

What was wrong with that answer? (*It was not true.*) The king had *not* sent him. Now David was in serious trouble. He chose to lie.

David wasn't the only visitor at the tabernacle that day. Doeg, one of King Saul's servants, heard everything David had said. What do you think he did? (*Immediately reported to Saul*)

From Nob, David fled to the city of Gath in Philistia. David had often fought against the Philistines. Now he was trying to find safety among them.

"You may stay here," said Achish, the king of Gath.

David thought everything was fine. He was safe. Then he overheard some soldiers talking to the king. "Don't you know who this is?" they asked. "This is David–the one who killed our man Goliath. He has slain thousands of our people."

David was terrified. *What can I do now?* he wondered. *Oh, what will I do?* David didn't think of asking God to help him.

Show Illustration #13

Instead, David pretended to be insane. He scratched on the gate with his hands. He let saliva run down his beard.

"Get him out of here!" the king shouted. "I have enough madmen around here! I do not need another."

David did escape. But what a terrible testimony he had been to that heathen king!

When David left Gath he hid in a big cave (Adullam). Now about 400 men joined him. They had not been happy with Saul. So they followed David.

Meanwhile, Doeg was reporting to King Saul. "I was in Nob, the city of the priests," he began. "David was there and asked for bread and a sword. He said you, O King, had sent him on urgent business."

Saul was furious! "Send for those priests immediately!" the king commanded.

Before long 86 priests stood before Saul. The king shouted, "Why are you taking sides with David and working against me?"

The high priest, Ahimelech, answered quietly. "Who, O King, is as faithful to you as David? He is honored in your household. He isn't against you."

King Saul did not want to hear the truth. He roared, "Ahimelech, you shall die!" He commanded his servants, "Kill all the priests! Go to Nob and kill their wives and children and all their animals."

Only Doeg was wicked enough to obey such an evil order.

One priest escaped and ran to tell David what had happened. David was heartbroken. "It is my fault!" he cried. "I am to blame for the death of all those people."

Think of how many innocent people suffered! Why? Because David–instead of trusting God–took matters into his own hands.

2. GOD PROTECTS DAVID
1 Samuel 23

David was still hiding in a cave. He had lots of time to think. He had learned some lessons the hard way. He had failed God miserably. He had hurt other people. He had lied. Could God ever use David again? (Let students respond. Emphasize the forgiveness which is available to all when we confess our sins. See Proverbs 28:13, 1 John 1:9.) Yes, God would be able to use David again, for he was truly sorry for his sins.

In the cave David thought a great deal about God. During this time he wrote Psalm 34. Listen to some of his thoughts: "I cried to the Lord, and He heard me and saved me from all my troubles." David prayed and God answered him (Psalm 34:6, 17, 19). "What a blessing to be able to run to the Lord and tell Him all my problems!" (Psalm 34:4, 8, 22) God is always waiting for His own to come to Him. He took away David's fear.

Together let us read Psalm 34:13 and 14. What had David learned about his lips and actions? (*The lie had he told resulted in death for many. His pretending to be insane was a terrible testimony to others.*)

David's troubles were not over. But David's heart was once again right with God. He was depending on the Lord to protect and guide him.

King Saul continued to hate David. He wanted to kill him. In fact, he sent spies throughout the country to look for David.

When they learned where David was, they reported to the king.

Show Illustration #14

Immediately, Saul and his army set out to capture David. David had no way to escape. The king's men surrounded him. The situation was hopeless. David knew he would be captured.

This time he did not take things into his own hands. Instead, he trusted God. And God did not fail him.

Right at that moment a messenger came running to Saul. "King Saul! The Philistines are raiding our land! You must help us!" God's timing was perfect. Saul forgot David and rushed home to fight his enemy, the Philistines.

Listen to David's song of praise: "The Lord is my Helper: He is my Friend!" (Psalm 54:4)

3. DAVID LOVES HIS ENEMY
1 Samuel 24, 26

"We must find a new place to hide," David told his men. "Saul knows where we are now. He will return as soon as he defeats the Philistines."

And that is exactly what the king did. Saul–along with 3,000 soldiers!–came looking for David. They searched up and down the hills. Where could David and his men be hiding?

All the time, David and his 600 followers were silently hiding, lying low, deep in the dark shadows of a huge cave (Engedi). They were breathless when Saul came right into the cave. But the king lay down and fell asleep. Imagine their amazement!

What could David do now? (*Kill Saul*) That is exactly what David's men whispered. "Here is your chance, David! Surely God sent Saul here so you can kill him. Then you will be rid of your enemy!"

Do you think David killed the king? Would you?

Listen! David tiptoed over to Saul and cut off the edge of his robe. But he did not touch the king. Without a sound, David returned to the shadows. He whispered to his men, "I should not have done this. Saul is the Lord's anointed king. We have no right to do anything against him."

David's men were amazed. They thought, *He could have killed Saul, but he let him go! This is unbelievable.*

Later Saul woke up and left the cave. David ran after him calling, "My lord the king!"

Show Illustration #15

Startled, Saul turned around. He saw David bowing to the ground to honor him.

David asked, "O King, why do you think I am trying to harm you?" Holding up the piece of Saul's garment, he said, "See! I was close enough to cut off a piece of your robe."

Looking down at his robe, Saul could see where David had cut it off.

"I could have cut off your head instead!" David continued. "But I don't want to kill you. I will never touch you because the Lord appointed you to be king."

Saul began to cry. Can you believe that? "Oh, David!" he cried. "You are much better than I. You could have killed me today. Instead, you spared my life. May the Lord reward you for what you have done. No one else would have been as kind to his enemy. I know you will be king one day. Please be kind to my children and grandchildren."

David promised Saul that he would. Saul returned to his palace. But David stayed in the caves. He simply didn't trust Saul.

As time went on, Saul let hatred and jealousy fill his thoughts. Forgetting David's love, he again went with his 3,000 men to destroy David.

This time David saw where Saul and his men were camping (Ziph). He waited until it was dark and all were sound asleep. Then he and one of his men, Abishai, slipped quietly into Saul's camp. They went right to the place where Saul was sleeping.

Abishai whispered to David, "God has delivered your enemy into your hand. Please let me kill him. I will strike him just once with the spear. He won't not suffer."

What do you think David said? (Read 1 Samuel 26:9.)

"Someday the Lord will take his life. Until then, I will not touch him," David said kindly. "We'll take his spear and his bottle of water. Hurry, let's go!"

Why do you think neither Saul nor any of his soldiers woke up? (Let students give suggestions. Read 1 Samuel 26:12b.) Once again the Lord God had protected David.

Safely away, atop a far-off hill, David shouted to Abner, Saul's bodyguard, "Abner! What kind of a guard are you?"

Aroused from sleep, Abner asked, "Who is calling?"

"I am!" answered David. "You deserve to be executed. You were sleeping instead of protecting the king. Do you know that someone came close enough to kill him? Where is his spear and his jug of water?"

Abner was terrified when he saw David holding high the spear and jug.

Saul woke up too. He heard David pleading with him: "Why do you track me down? What wrong have I done?"

Again Saul confessed that he was wrong. "Please come back to the palace with me, David. I will never, never again try to harm you," he promised.

Did David go? No! He knew King Saul couldn't be trusted. Nevertheless, David loved and respected the king. God alone could give David such a kind attitude.

4. DAVID MOURNS
1 Samuel 31; 2 Samuel 1

One day while in battle against the Philistines Saul was badly wounded. He knew he was going to die. Saul didn't want his enemies to kill him. So he killed himself with his own sword. What a sad end! In that same battle Saul's son Jonathan was also killed.

Do you think David was happy when he heard that Saul was dead? He wouldn't have to hide anymore. He would no longer need to be afraid. He would be the new king of Israel! Did he rejoice when a messenger brought the news to him?

Show Illustration #16

No! Instead, David tore his clothes. This was a sign of mourning. He cried all day and refused to eat. He even wrote a song about Saul and Jonathan. (See 2 Samuel 1:19-27.)

David was a godly man. His heart was right with God. God helped him to show kindness to others–even to his enemy.

Is there someone who is unkind to you? Maybe that person doesn't hurt you physically. But does he hurt you with lies and unkind deeds? How do you treat that person? Have you learned from David how you should react? (Let students share lessons they have learned.) Who can help us to love those who do not love us? *(God)*

The Bible tells us we are to love others as we love ourselves. (See Matthew 22:39.) That is how David loved Saul. He could have hated him and sought revenge. Instead, God won his battles for him.

God loved you even when you were as hateful and wicked as Saul. Many years after the death of Saul, God sent His Son, the Lord Jesus, to die for you. (See Romans 5:8.) If you will receive the Lord Jesus Christ, God will forgive your wickedness. He will cleanse your heart and make you His own child.

www.ingramcontent.com/pod-product-compliance
Lightning Source LLC
Chambersburg PA
CBHW060801090426
42736CB00002B/115